The rhyme gives children extra help with predicting the next word or phrase. By pausing as you read, you are making space for children to contribute what they know and remember.

A noisy newt and an owl on a chair
A big pig pattering …

here and there …

I spy with my little eye a kangaroo, a leopard and a monkey – k l m.

I Spy ABC encourages children to notice the links between letters and sounds in an enjoyable and meaningful way.

At my party I'd have ice-cream and an enormous birthday cake like that.

That sounds nice!

Children often learn more about a story through talking about it. It may remind them of events in their own lives.

We hope you enjoy reading this book together.

For lovely Lisa with hugs from Viv
V.F.

For Ken
S.H.

First published 1998 by Walker Books Ltd
87 Vauxhall Walk, London SE11 5HJ

8 10 9 7

Text © 1998 Vivian French
Illustrations © 1998 Sally Holmes
Introductory and concluding notes © 1998 CLPE/LB Southwark

Printed in Hong Kong

ISBN 0-7445-4886-1

I SPY
ABC

Vivian French

Illustrated by
Sally Holmes

WALKER BOOKS
AND SUBSIDIARIES
LONDON • BOSTON • SYDNEY

I spy with my little eye. . .

An **antelope** in a coat and tie
A flittery, fluttery **butterfly**

A **crocodile** beginning to cry
And a **dinosaur** go dancing by.

What do I spy with my eye today?
An elegant **elephant** all in grey
A fine fat **frog** that's lost her way
Grandfather **grasshopper** down in the hay
And a dinosaur go hurrying by.

What can I spy? What can I see?
A hungry **hedgehog** under a tree
An **iguana** itching his knee
A **jellyfish** jumping out of the sea
And a dinosaur go leaping by.

What can I see? What can I spy?
A **kangaroo** skipping right up to the sky
A **leopard** singing a lullaby

Monkeys munching a piece of pie
And the dinosaur go waddling by.

What do I see? What's over there?
A noisy **newt** and an **owl** on a chair
A big **pig** pattering here and there
A **quail** that's quietly pecking a pear
And the dinosaur go stomping by.

I can see in a wink and a blink
A **reindeer** slide on a skating rink
A **seal** that sits in the kitchen sink
A **tiger** twirling his tail to drink
And the dinosaur go puffing by.

What can I see? What can I do?
There's only **unicorn** left for U
A **vole** who doesn't know what to do
A **whale** that wallows in seas of blue
And the dinosaur go paddling by.

I spy with my little eye
An **x-ray fish** swim quickly by
A stamping, tramping yackety **yak**
A **zebra** dressed in white and black ...

And there's the dinosaur dancing back!

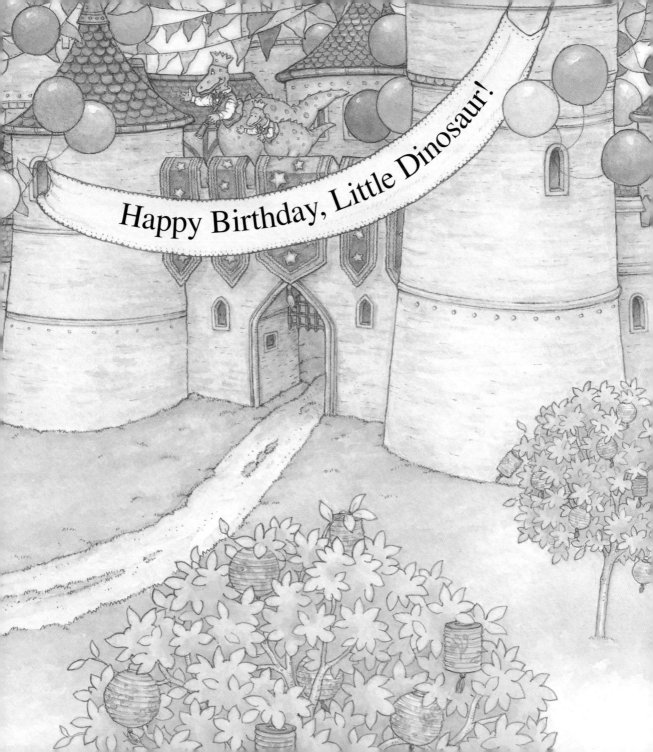

Happy Birthday, Little Dinosaur!

Dd Dinosaur

Ee Elephant

Ff Frog

Jj Jellyfish

Kk Kangaroo

Ll Leopard

Qq Quail

Rr Reindeer

Ss Seal

Tt Tiger

Xx X-ray fish

Yy Yak

Zz Zebra

Read it again

Spot the animal
Looking through the book together
you and your child can choose
a letter and find the animal
beginning with that letter
both in the pictures and
in the words.

There's the elephant!

And here's "e" for elephant

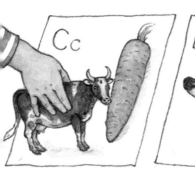

I spy with my little eye
Children can play an "I Spy" game,
grouping toy animals or food together,
or sticking pictures of objects on to big
sheets of paper with letters on them.
A good way to start is by using letters
of family names.

Make an alphabet book
Children can be helped to make
their own alphabet book of
friends and family names
or of familiar objects.
Encourage them to write
any names or letters they
know and then
help write
in the rest.

Henry's here and Sophie and Mr Floppy and Baby Bear.

Party invitations

Throughout the book, the little dinosaur has been delivering birthday party invitations to all his friends. You could help your child to make up their own party list, either for their birthday or for a pretend celebration with their favourite toys.

ABCDEFG HIJK ...

LMNOP!

Singing the alphabet

Turn back a page and use the cards to encourage your child to sing their way through the alphabet. It's one of the best ways to help them remember.

Other alphabet books

There's a huge variety of alphabet books available in bookshops, libraries and supermarkets. Talking through them together is a valuable way for children to get to know about letters and sounds and learn the alphabet.

Reading Together

The *Reading Together* series is divided into four levels – starting with red, then on to yellow, blue and finally green. The six books in each level offer children varied experiences of reading. There are stories, poems, rhymes and songs, traditional tales and information books to choose from.

Accompanying the series is a Parents' Handbook, which looks at all the different ways children learn to read and explains how *your* help can really make a difference!